Calvin Stowell

**Statutes of the imperial, ecclesiastical, military and masonic**

**order of the Knights of the Red Cross**

1559

Calvin Stowell

**Statutes of the imperial, ecclesiastical, military and masonic order of the Knights of the Red Cross**
*1559*

ISBN/EAN: 9783337257279

Printed in Europe, USA, Canada, Australia, Japan

Cover: Foto ©ninafisch / pixelio.de

More available books at **www.hansebooks.com**

# STATUTES

—OF THE—

## Imperial, Ecclesiastical, Military and Masonic Order

— OF —

# Knights of the Red Cross of Constantine

## AND APPENDANT ORDERS

— OF THE —

## Grand Council of the State of Pennsylvania,

ADOPTED

**READING, JUNE 14, A D. 1872, A. O. 1559,**

— WITH —

## BY-LAWS FOR SUBORDINATE CONCLAVES,

*FORMS OF VARIOUS KINDS,*

AND TO WHICH IS PREFIXED

A Sketch of the History of the Order and its Introduction into the United States.

———— ·•· ————

Most Illustrious Sir CALVIN L. STOWELL, Grand Sovereign, Rouseville, Venango County, Pa.
Illustrious Sir ALFRED CREIGH, Grand Recorder, Washington, Washington County, Pa.

———— ·•· ————

HARRISBURG, PA.
THEO. F. SCHEFFER, PRINTER.
1872.

# Masonic Order of the Red Cross of Constantine.

---

*Declaration of the principles of the above Order, written in 1806, by the late Judge Waller Rodwell Wright, then M. I. Grand Master of the Order, and R. W. Provincial Grand Master for the Ionian Islands, under the Grand Lodge of England.*

"The Order of the Red Cross is one of those numerous branches of Chivalry which had their origin in the holy Wars, and the distinction worn by its Knights was the original badge of the Crusaders in general.

"As this Order never was endowed with particular revenues, its members were for the most part persons of independent condition, or associated with one of the great Sovereign Orders of the Temple, or St. John of Jerusalem.

"As, however, the distinguishing characteristic and constitutions of this Order, though existing only in unwritten tradition, have been partially preserved to the present age, some Knights Templar, zealous in the united cause of Masonry and chivalry, have thought it expedient to revive it, on the footing of its ancient establishment, and that for various reasons:—

"*First.* Because the original intent of the Masonic Institution has been greatly frustrated by the indiscriminate admission of persons of every description and character.

"*Second.* Because it unfortunately happens that the sublime branch of our system known by the denomination of Christian Masonry has fallen into still worse hands, whereby the Test of Faith originally required of the Candidates for initiation has been dispensed with, the rites and mysteries of the Order degraded, and selection rendered indispensably necessary.

"*Thirdly.* And this, indeed, is the most powerful reason which has induced them to bring forward this ancient Order. They earnestly wish to counteract the evil designs to which the privileges of the Masonic system have been perverted by men of unprincipled character, and to combat the enemies of Christianity and social order by the same secret and powerful means which they have made use of to effect their purposes.

"The objects, therefore, of the Red Cross are these:—

"To draw closer the bond of Masonic union, purify the system of Masonic science, extend its limits, and increase its influence by combining such of its professors as are best qualified by character and principle, respectability and influence, genius and talent, to effectuate this great purpose.

"To prevent the perversion of its institutions and privileges to objects contrary to, and abhorrent from its original intent.

"To combat infidelity and treason under whatever form existing, and promote by every humble means the social happiness and eternal welfare of our fellow-creatures.

"It is therefore necessary:—

"That we observe the greatest circumspection in the choice of our members and associates.

"That we adhere inviolably and scrupulously to the principles and constitutions of our Order.

"That we cultivate a strict and fraternal union among ourselves.

"And that we on all occasions give our decided preference to intellectual and moral excellence over every other consideration whatsoever."

I hereby certify that the manuscript of which the above is a verbatim extract is one of the documents relating to the Red Cross Order, which were found in the archives of the Grand Lodge of England, and handed over by command of the Right Honorable the Earl of Zetland P. G. M., then M. W. Grand Master, to Lord Kenlis, the head of the Order of the Red Cross in England.

JOHN HERVEY, (P. S. G. Deacon,)
*Grand Secretary of the United Grand Lodge of England.*
Freemason's Hall, London,
    *1st Sept. 1870.*

# Memorabilia of the Order.

A. D. 313. Foundation of the Order, by Constantine the Great.

" 326. Foundation of the Order of Knights of the Holy Sepulchre, by St. Helena, the mother of Constantine.

" 1099. Revival of the Red Cross and K. H. S. Orders amongst the Crusaders.

" 1190. The Order of Constantine revived.

" 1750. The Order first alluded to in connection with Freemasonry, by the Baron Hunde in his Templar System of "Strict Observance."

" 1788. The Order conferred in England by Sir Charles Shirreff, a Deputy Grand Inspector General of the Scottish Rite.

" 1796. The Right Honorable Lord Rancliffe elected Grand Master of the Red Cross Order and K. H. S.

" 1804. Hon. Waller Rodwell Wright, Esq., elected Grand Master.

" 1809. Sir William Henry White, Esq , installed Grand Secretary.

" 1810. The Grand Seal of the Order adopted.

" 1811. Sir Richard Jebb, Esq.. empowered to create Knights in British India.

" 1813. Annual subscription first introduced.

" 1813. H. R. H., the Duke of Sussex installed and elected Grand Sovereign.

" 1813. Costume and regalia adopted.

" 1813. A sword, which cost one hundred guineas, presented to Sir. W. H. Wright, on his retirement from the Sovereignty of the Order.

" 1814. Intendants General appointed.

" 1843. Death of H. R. H., the Duke of Sussex.

" 1862. Original Conclave revived.

" 1865. The Grand Council revived. Election of Sir Wm. Henry White as Grand Sovereign. He died in 1866.

" 1866. Lord Kenlis (now Earl of Bective) elected Grand Sovereign.

" 1868. Lord Kenlis re-elected at the second triennial assembly.

" 1869. The Order introduced into the Dominion of Canada, by Sir W. J. B. McLeod Moore, who was appointed Chief Inspector General.

A. D. 1870. Sept. 30.—The Order introduced into Pennsylvania by Sir Alfred Creigh, who was appointed a Divisional Inspector General.

    1871. January 1.—Sir Alfred Creigh was commissioned Chief Intendant General for the State of Pennsylvania and for all other States in the American Union, by the Earl of Bective.

    1871. Third Triennial Assembly held in England, and the Earl of Bective re-elected.

    " 1871. The Order introduced into Nebraska.

    " 1871. The Order introduced into New York by Sir C. L. Stowell, a Divisional Inspector General.

    " 1871. The Order introduced into Illinois by Sir J. J. French, M. D., a Divisional Inspector General.

    " 1871. The rank of Past Grand Viceroy of the Grand Council of England was conferred upon Sir Alfred Creigh.

    " 1872. Sir Alfred Creigh, Chief Intendant General of the United States, appointed the following Intendants General, viz: Sir Calvin L. Stowell, for Pennsylvania; Sir J. J. French, for Illinois; Sir A. G. Goodall, for New York; Sir D. Burnham Tracy, for Michigan.

    " 1872. The Order introduced into Michigan.

    " 1872. The Grand Council of Pennsylvania organized at Reading, June 14.

    " 1872. The Order introduced into Massachusetts. Sir N. G. Tucker appointed an Intendant General for Massachusetts and Rhode Island.

    1872. The Grand Council of Illinois organized at Chicago, August 30.

# HISTORY.

After the memorable battle fought at Saxa Rubra, on the 28th of October, A. D. 313, the Emperor Constantine sent for the Chiefs of the Christian legion, and, (we here quote the words of an old ritual,) in the presence of his other officers, constituted them into an Order of Knighthood, and appointed them to wear the form of the cross he had seen in the heavens upon their shields, with the motto *In hoc signo vinces* round it, surrounded with clouds. He became the sovereign patron of the Christian Order of the Red Cross.

This cross was ordered to be embroidered upon all the imperial standards. The Christian warriors were selected by Constantine as his body guard, and the command of these soldiers of the cross was confided to Eusebius, Bishop of Nicomedia, who was thus considered the Viceroy, or second in command.

After the death of Constantine, the Order flourished during the reigns of Marcian and Leo I; but its history is enshrouded somewhat, until the year 1190, when it was revived by the Emperor Isaac Angelus Comnenus on a scale of magnificent splendor.

From 1190 to 1699, the Grand Mastership was vested in the Comnenus family, who were considered the lineal descendants of Constantine; and on the resignation of Andrew Angelus Flavius Comnenus, Francis Farnese, the reigning Duke of Parma, became his successor.

The Abbe Giuistiniani, who was attached to the Venetian embassy in London, conferred, by authority, the Order in England; but at what precise time it became restricted to Freemasons we cannot positively state.

In 1788, many distinguished Freemasons and Knights Templar were admitted, and among the number, a majority of the grand officers of the various Masonic grand bodies of England. Lord Rancliffe, Grand Master of the Templars, Judge Waller Rodwell Wright, Provincial Grand Master for the Ionian Islands, and a personal friend of the Dukes of Sussex and Kent, were among the permanent and active members of the Illustrious Order in 1796.

In 1808, the written history shows a revival in the Order, by the introduction of some of the most distinguished Templars and Masons, among whom are Earls, Lords, Dukes, Ministers, &c.

Year after year, from this period, we find the Order increasing in dignity, efficiency in numerical strength, until his Royal Highness the Duke of Sussex was unanimously elected Grand Master of the Order, for and during his natural life, in 1813.

In this year, the two Grand Lodges of England entered into articles of union, and among the articles, we quote the second, which reads thus: "It is declared and pronounced that pure and ancient Masonry consists of three degrees, and no more, viz: those of E. A., F. C., and M. M., including the Supreme Order of the Holy Royal Arch." *But this article is not intended to prevent any Lodge or Chapter from holding a meeting in any of the degrees of the Orders of Chivalry, according to the Constitution of the said Orders.*

For the information of our members, we will state that the KNIGHTS TEMPLAR, KNIGHTS OF THE RED CROSS, and KNIGHTS OF THE HOLY SEPULCHRE were the only organized Chivalric Orders existing in England at the time of the Union, in 1813, and, consequently, the above permissive clause applies *solely* to their members.

From that time forward the Order has flourished, and no disturbance has taken place among the brethren—it being under the Grand Mastership of the Earl of Bective.

We now come to its introduction into the UNITED STATES.

After much correspondence had taken place between the Eminent and Illustrious Sir W. J. B. McLeod Moore, of La Prairie, Canada, and Chief Inspector General of Knights of the Red Cross, and Lord Kenlis, in regard to the introduction of these Christian and Chivalric Orders into the United States, the following letter was forwarded to Sir Alfred Creigh, with whom Sir W. J. B. McLeod Moore, Chief Inspector General, had been in correspondence on the subject:

> LA PRAIRIE, PROVINCE OF QUEBEC,
> DOMINION OF CANADA, *November 2, 1872.*

MOST EMINENT AND PERFECT KNIGHT:

It affords me pleasure to inform you that the Most Puissant the Grand Sovereign of the Order of Red Cross of Rome and Constantine in England, the Right Honorable Lord Kenlis, has fully authorized me, by letter from the Grand Recorder of the Order, Illustrious Sir Knight Robt. Wentworth Little, dated London, 16th February, 1870, to introduce this Chivalric and Christian Order into the United States of America, premising that, until the Order is sufficiently established, the United States Knights must hold under England; but should the Order spread in the United States of America, they can remain in full union with the Grand Council of England or obtain Grand Councils of their own, in fraternity with England, as they please. Having now obtained from you the preliminary vow, signed by yourself and eleven other worthy and illustrious brethren, Sir Knights of the Order of the Temple, I hereby forward you the authorized rituals of the three grades of the Order, together with a commission to establish the Order in the State of Pennsylvania, United States of America.

The whole of the petitioning Knights, who have signed the vow, can receive the three grades; and on the formation of new Conclaves, until the Order is fully established, you can confer the second or Viceroy grade on *seven* of the Knights, and the third grade or that of Honorary Sovereign on *three* of the Knights.

Wishing you every success in the establishment of the Imperial, Ecclesiastical and Military Order of the Red Cross of Rome and Constantine in the State of Pennsylvania.

I am ever,

Most Eminent and Perfect Knight.

Most fraternally yours,

W. J. B. McLEOD MOORE,

*Chief Inspector General of Canada and Representative of Gr. Council of England.*

With this letter was forwarded the enclosed commission, which reads as follows:

LA PRAIRIE, PROVINCE OF QUEBEC, DOMINION OF CANADA.

THIS IS TO CERTIFY, That the very enlightened and perfect Knight Alfred Creigh, 33°, (an L. L. D.,) of Washington, Washington county, Pennsylvania, United States of America, is, by the authority invested in me, as the representative of the Grand Council of the Order of the Red Cross of Rome and Constantine in England, authorized to introduce and establish this *Imperial, Ecclesiastical and Military Order* into the State of Pennsylvania, United States of America.

*And further,* That the aforesaid Very Eminent and Perfect Knight Alfred Creigh is hereby commissioned by me and appointed a *Divisional Inspector General* of the Order in the said State of Pennsylvania.

Given under my hand and seal of arms, this 30th day of September, A. L. 5874, A. D. 1870. A. O. 1557.

W. J. B. McLEOD MOORE,

*Chief Insp. Gen. K. R. C. of Canada.*

Upon the receipt of this commission, Sir Alfred Creigh organized Conclaves in Washington, Bloomsburg, Reading, Harrisburg, and Allentown. But on the 1st of January, 1871, his authority was enlarged by a commission direct from England, which reads as follows.

*Initium Sapientiæ Amor Domini.*

## IN THE NAME OF THE MOST GLORIOUS TRINITY IN UNITY.

**From the East in London, a Place full of Light, wherein reign Silence and Peace but Darkness comprehendeth it not.**

*To whom it may concern, Greeting, but more especially to the Knights Companion of the Imperial, Ecclesiastical and Military Order of the Red Cross of Rome and Constantine, the Invincible Order of Knights of the Holy Sepulchre and the Holy Order of St. John :*

FAITH.                    UNITY.                    ZEAL.

KNOW YE, That, in consideration of the great trust and confidence we repose in our well-beloved Companion, the Illustrious Sir Knight ALFRED CREIGH, L. L. D., of Washington, Washington county, Pennsylvania, United States of America, we do hereby delegate him as our representative, and appoint him our *Intendant General for the State of Pennsylvania and for all other States in the American Union,* for which there is no Intendant General commissioned ; and the Illustrious Knight Alfred Creigh is hereby empowered to instal Master Masons of good repute as members of the aforesaid Illustrious Order the of Red Cross, for the purpose of forming new Conclaves ; and further authorized to inspect such Conclaves when established, and to hear and decide upon all matters affecting the well being of the Order, subject, nevertheless, to appeal to our supreme adjudication and determination.

*Provided, also,* That the said Illustrious Knight shall transmit, or cause to be transmitted, to us, Thomas, Earl of Bective, or to the Most Eminent Sir Frederick Martin Williams, Baronet, Member of Parliament for Truro, our Grand Viceroy or Eusebius, or to the Most Illustrious Grand Sovereign or Grand Viceroy for the time being, all returns, fees and payments on behalf of the members of such Conclaves, now er hereafter to be established in the said State of Pennsylvania and all other States in the American Union for which there is no Intendant General commissioned, as may be required by the general statutes or the edicts of the Grand Imperial Council. Otherwise this our commission shall cease to be of any force or virtue, and become absolutely null and void.

And we pray the Omnipotent Ruler of the Universe to have the said Illustrious Knight Alfred Creigh in His most holy keeping.

Given at our Grand Council Chamber, Freemasons' Tavern, London, and sealed with the Seals of the aforesaid Orders of the Red Cross and Knights of the Holy Sepulchre, this 1st day of January, A. M. 5875, A. D. 1871, A. O. 1558.

BECTIVE,
*Grand Sovereign.*

[SEAL.]        [SEAL.]

FRED'K M. WILLIAMS,
*Gr. V. or Eusebius.*

ATTEST:— R. WENTWORTH LITTLE,
*Gr. Recorder.*

As we have given the authority upon which the Order was introduced into the United States, although the commission states that it may be conferred upon Master Masons, yet those who were instrumental in its introduction, learning that it was purely Christian in its character, resolved that it should be confined to those who had taken the Commandery degrees. To settle, therefore, this fact, we will call the attention of the Sir Knights to the letter of Nov. 2, 1870, from Sir Moore, in which he states "that having now received the preliminary vow, signed by yourself and eleven other worthy and illustrious brethren, *Sir Knights of the Order of the Temple*, I forward you the authorized rituals. The diploma which each Sir Knight receives from England, commences with these words: "In the name of the Most Holy and Blessed Trinity and Unity." So also, in a 'etter from the Grand Recorder Little, dated July 8. 1872, writes: " *The rule you have adopted as to restricting the Order in the States to Templars is doubtless a wise and salutary one.*" and is in accordance with the declaration of principles. as contained on pages 3 and 4.

We now proceed with our history.

On the 23rd of May, 1871. Sir R. Wentworth Little, Grand Recorder, wrote to the Eminent Sir Alfred Creigh that it was the request of the Earl of Bective, Grand Sovereign of the Order, that he should assume the title of "*Chief Intendant General* for the Northern Jurisdiction of the United States of America."

On October 4, 1871, the rank of Past Grand Viceroy of the Grand Council of England was conferred upon the Eminent and Illustrious Alfred Creigh, for his faithful and meritorious services.

On December 27, 1871. the Grand Recorder Little informs Sir Creigh, the Chief Intendant General of the Northern Jurisdiction, that the Order of Red Cross of Constantine and Appendant Orders cannot be introduced into any of the American States without the Chief Intendant's General sanction; that he being the appointed chief, all business of the Order must be transacted through him.

February 5, 1872, Sir Alfred Creigh, Chief Intendant General, was authorized to appoint Intendants General for each State in which no Independent State Grand Council was organized, and under that authority he appointed Eminent and Illustrious Sir C. L. Stowell, for Pennsylvania; Eminent and Illustrious Sir J. J. French, for Illinois; Eminent and Illustrious Sir A. G. Goodall, for New York; Eminent and Illustrious D. Burnham Tracy, for Michigan; and Sir N. G. Tucker, for Massachusetts and Rhode Island.

At a preliminary meeting of the officers of the various Councils organized in Pennsylvania, and held December 5th, 1871. in Philadelphia, it was

*Resolved,* That application should be made, through Sir Alfred Creigh, to establish an Independent State Grand Body.

And. on the 25th of January. 1872, the following authority was issued :

WHEREAS, It has been represented to me. by our trusty and well-beloved Frater Sir Knight Alfred Creigh, L. I. D.. Chief Intendant General of the Order for the *United States of America,* that it will conduce to the stability and prosperity of the Order in Pennsylvania, if the Knights resident in that State be permitted to organize an Independent Grand Council for Pennsylvania:

*Know ye, all whom it may concern,* That we, Thomas, Earl of Bective, Grand Sovereign, do hereby authorize and empower the aforesaid Sir Knight Alfred Creigh to take such measures as may seem to him expedient for the organization and permanent establishment of a Grand Council for the State of Pennsylvania : *Provided,* that the consent of a majority of the representatives of the Conclaves now existing within the limits of the State be signified. after due notice and in conformity with these presents.

And we charge the aforesaid Knight to make known to us, for the information of our Grand Council, all the proceedings which shall be taken in reference to the formation of the Grand Council of Pennsylvania, hereby confirming him as our special representative and Chief Intendant General for ALL the States of the American Union. until Independent Grand Councils shall be organized in each State.

Herewith we have subscribed our name and affixed the Seal of our Grand Council.

[SEAL.]                              BECTIVE,
                                    *Grand Sovereign.*

In accordance with this authority, circulars were issued to the following conclaves, then in existence in Pennsylvania. viz: U. S. Premier Conclave, No. 38. at Washington ; Orient Conclave, No. 45. at Bloomsburg, Constantine, No. 46, at Reading ; Trinity, No. 47, at Harrisburg ; Mary, No. 48, at Allentown ; Bellefonte, No. 51. at Bellefonte ; Allegheny, No. 53, at Allegheny ; Philadelphia No. 57. at Philadelphia ; Earl of Bective, No. 58. at Towanda ; Red Rose, No. 59. at Columbia ; Rose of Sharon, No. 60, at Rouseville ; Corry, No. 71, at Corry ; Sage Conclave, No. 74, at Franklin ; and Lilly of the Valley. No. 75. at Titusville ; which gave their consent as prescribed to the formation of a Grand Council, and the 14th day of June, 1872. was designated. and the city of Reading. as the place of meeting.

# PROCEEDINGS.

———◆◆◆———

The meeting was called to order by the Eminent and Illustrious Sir Alfred Creigh. Chief Intendant General—when the following Eminent Knights produced their credentials, viz :

Conclave 38, M. P. ALFRED CREIGH.
     "   45,   "   C. F. KNAPP, CHAS. R. EARLEY.
     "   46.   "   J. C. A. HOFFEDITZ. B. F. HAGEY.
     "   47.   "   THEO. F. SCHEFFER.
     "   48,   "   D. J. MARTIN, per proxy.
     "   51.   "   D. F. BUSH, per proxy.
     "   57.   "   C. E. MEYER, J. L. YOUNG.
         58,      H. B. McKEAN, per proxy.
     "   59.      A. J. KAUFMAN, per proxy.
     "   60.      C. L. STOWELL.
     "   71.   "   B. C. PHELPS. per proxy.
     "   74.      M W. SAGE.
     "   75.      A. A. ASPINSALL, per proxy.

Eminent and Illustrious Sir J. J. FRENCH M. D., Divisional Inspector General of Illinois, was admitted and received with the honors appertaining to his office. All the conclaves except one being represented, the Chief Intendant General called M. P. Sovereign, C. F. KNAPP to the chair, and Eminent ALFRED CREIGH was appointed Recorder.

The commission of the Earl of Bective to organize an Independent Grand Council of Masonic Knights of the Red Cross of Constantine and the Appendant Orders was then read.

On motion of Eminent Sir C. L. STOWELL,

*Resolved*, That we, the representatives of the various conclaves in the State of Pennsylvania, acting under charters derived from the most Illustrious Grand Council of England, do hereby form ourselves into an Independent Grand Council of Masonic Knights of the Red Cross of Constantine and the Appendant Orders for the State of Pennsylvania.

On motion of Eminent Sir C. E. MEYER,

*Resolved,* That we adopt the new constitution of the Grand Commandery of Knights Templar, as far as applicable to this Grand Council and
that the most Illustrious Grand Master and Grand Recorder be and
they are hereby authorized to make the same conform to the General
Statutes of the Grand Council of England.

On motion of Eminent Sir THEO. F. SCHEFFER,

*Resolved,* That we proceed to the election of officers, which resulted as
follows :

| | |
|---|---|
| Most Illustrious CALVIN L. STOWELL, | Grand Sovereign. |
| Most Illustrious CHRISTIAN F KNAPP, | Grand Viceroy or Eusebius. |
| Very Illustrious JOHN L YOUNG, | Grand Senior General. |
| "    THEO. F. SCHEFFER, | Grand Junior General. |
| CHARLES R. EARLEY, | Grand High Prelate. |
| "    MILES W. SAGE. | Grand High Chancellor. |
| "    J. C. A. HOFFEDITZ, | Grand Treasurer. |
| "    ALFRED CREIGH. | Grand Recorder. |

Whereupon the Eminent and Illustrious Sir ALFRED CREIGH, Chief Intendant General of the United States, administered to each officer the
usual vow and charges appertaining to their respective offices, and con-
gratulated the Sir Knights on the organization of the *first* Grand Council
established in the United States.

On motion of Eminent Sir CHARLES R. EARLEY,

*Resolved,* That Sir ALFRED CREIGH, Chief Intendant General, be requested to write the history of the Order, with the facts connected with
its introduction into the United States, and incorporate therein the necessary documents in regard to the organization of this Grand Council.

On motion of Eminent Sir CHRISTIAN F. KNAPP,

*Resolved,* That the working degrees of the Order shall be: 1. Knight
of the Red Cross of Constantine; 2. Knight of the Holy Sepulchre;
3. Knight of St. John; and the degrees of Most Puissant Sovereign and
Viceroy shall be recognized as official degrees and conferred as the Constitution shall direct.

On motion of Eminent Sir MILES W. SAGE,

*Resolved,* That all Knight companions who have up to this date received the degrees of M. P. Sovereign and Viceroy in any subordinate
Conclave, and who have not filled these offices by election, be recognized
as honorary members of this Grand Council, but not entitled to vote on
any question.

On motion of Eminent Sir Charles E. Meyer,

*Resolved*, That the charters now in possession of the Conclaves issued by the Grand Council of England, be indorsed by the M. P. Grand Sovereign and Illustrious Grand Recorder, with the seal attached, and numbered according to their respective dates, and it shall be the duty of the M. P. Sovereign of each Conclave to forward the charter to the Grand Officers designated for this purpose.

*Resolved*, That all business transacted in subordinate Conclaves shall be done in the order of Knights of the Holy Sepulchre, and that each Conclave shall "open" and "close" in that order.

*Resolved*, That the blank forms and ceremonies used by the Grand Imperial Council of England be adopted by this Grand Council.

*Resolved*, That the regalia, badges and jewels of the Order as set forth, and now in use by the Grand Imperial Council of England be adopted for the same purpose by the Grand Council of Pennsylvania.

On motion of Eminent Sir John L. Young.

*Resolved*, That the Most Illustrious Grand Sovereign shall have the prerogative and power to appoint *Divisional Intendants General* for Pennsylvania, and also without regard to number.

*Resolved*, That the Most Illustrious Grand Sovereign can confer the Orders "at sight" for the purpose of organizing new Conclaves, and that the fees thereof be returned to this Grand Council, the minimum in such cases being $10 per each member.

*Resolved*, That subordinate Conclaves shall pay to the Grand Council for each member installed, $2 as an initiation fee, and for a certificate of membership which said sum shall be forwarded by the Recorder of each subordinate Conclave to the Grand Recorder within three days, who shall issue said certificate immediately.

*Resolved*, That subordinate Conclaves shall pay to the Grand Council twenty-five cents per annum, for each member.

On motion of Eminent Sir Christian F. Knapp,

*Resolved*, That the Grand Recorder furnish the names of each Grand Officer of this Grand Council and the M. P. Sovereign of each Conclave to the Chief Intendant General of the United States, to be forwarded to the Grand Imperial Council of England for the decoration of the Grand Cross of the Order and that hereafter the Order of the Grand Cross shall not be conferred upon any one who has not been approved by a two-thirds vote of the Grand Council.

*Resolved*, That the Constitutional qualification shall require all applicants for admission into the Order to be Knights Templar in good standing.

*Resolved*, That each Conclave shall have permission, if they so desire, to hold a new election for officers, but hereafter said election shall be held at the regular meeting, next preceding St. John's day in December.

*Resolved*, That the Very Eminent Sir WILLIAM JAMES HUGHAN, of Truro Cornwall, England, be appointed the Representative for the Grand Council of Pennsylvania, near the Grand Imperial Council of England, and that the Grand Council of England be requested to appoint as their Representative near the Grand Council of Pennsylvania, Eminent Sir Alfred Creigh.

The Most Illustrious Grand Sovereign was pleased to make the following appointments:

Eminent Sir WM. C. TYLER,        Illustrious Grand Chamberlain.
"       DEWEES J. MARTIN,        "        "    Orator.
"       WM. H EGLE,              "              Marshal.
"       H. C. L. CRECELIUS,      "             Sentinel.

Also, the Most Illustrious Sir CHRISTIAN F. KNAPP and the Eminent Sir CHARLES E. MEYER, Divisional Intendants General.

*Resolved*, That the M P. Illustrious Grand Sovereign issue a circular to the subordinate Conclaves, requesting the M. P. Sovereign of each Conclave, to collect from each Sir Knight fifty cents to pay necessary expenses, and that the M. P. Grand Sovereign and Illustrious Grand Recorder be authorized to have three hundred copies of the History and proceedings published.

*Resolved*, That the M P. Grand Sovereign and Illustrious Grand Recorder procure a seal, books, &c., necessary to be had.

The Most Illustrious Grand Council of Knights of the Red Cross of Constantine was closed in ample form, to meet in Allentown, Lehigh county, on the Thursday after the 2nd Wednesday of February, A. D. 1873, A. O. 1560, at 8 o'clock, P. M.

ALFRED CREIGH,
*Grand Recorder.*

# STATUTES

OF THE

# Grand Council of Pennsylvania.

## STATUTE I.

### OF THE GRAND COUNCIL.

SEC. 1. This body shall be styled THE GRAND COUNCIL OF KNIGHTS OF THE RED CROSS OF CONSTANTINE AND THE APPENDANT ORDERS OF PENNSYLVANIA.

SEC. 2. The Grand Council consists of the following members, and rank in the following order, viz:

    I. The Most Illustrious Grand Sovereign.

    II. The Most Illustrious Grand Viceroy or Eusebius.

    III. The Very Illustrious Grand Senior General.

    IV. The Very Illustrious Grand Junior General.

    V. The Very Illustrious Grand High Prelate.

    VI. Illustrious Grand High Chancellor.

    VII. The Illustrious Grand Treasurer.

    VIII. The Illustrious Grand Recorder.

    IX. The Illustrious Grand Chamberlain.

    X. The Illustrious Grand Orator.

    XI. The Illustrious Grand Marshal.

    XII. The Illustrious Grand Sentinel.

LIKEWISE,

    XIII. All Past Grand Sovereigns.

XIV.  All Past Grand Viceroys.

   So long as they remain members of subordinate
   Conclaves under this jurisdiction.

LIKEWISE,

XV.  The M. P. Sovereign, and

XVI.  The Viceroy or Eusebius,

   Of each chartered subordinate Conclave working
   under this Grand Council.

LIKEWISE,

XVII.  All Past M. P. Sovereigns of the subordinate Conclaves working under this Grand Council, so long
as they remain members of subordinate Conclaves
under this jurisdiction.

SEC. 3.  Each of the individuals enumerated in this section shall
be entitled, when present, to one vote.

SEC. 4.  No Knight shall be eligible to office in this Grand
Council, unless he shall be at the time a member of some subordinate Conclave working under this jurisdiction, and a Past Sovereign.

The *Elective* officers of this Grand Council are chosen by ballot,
and shall consist of—

   I.  A Most Illustrious Grand Sovereign.

   II.  A Most Illustrious Grand Viceroy or Eusebius.

   III.  A Very Illustrious Grand Senior General.

   IV.  A Very Illustrious Grand Junior General.

   V.  A Very Illustrious Grand High Prelate.

   VI.  A Very Illustrious Grand High Chancellor.

   VII.  An Illustrious Grand Treasurer.

   VIII.  An Illustrious Grand Recorder.

The other officers shall be appointed by the Most Illustrious
Grand Sovereign elect.

## STATUTE II.

### PROXIES.

SEC. 1.  Any officer specified in Statute I, save and except Past

Sovereigns, may appear and vote by proxy, said proxy being at the time of service a member of the same subordinate Conclave as his principal, and producing a properly authenticated certificate of his appointment.

Sec. 2. None but members of the Grand Council who are entitled to vote shall be allowed to be present during the election of officers.

## STATUTE III.

### COUNCILS.

Sec. 1. The Grand Council shall be held annually, on the Thursday after the second Wednesday of February in each and every year, and be opened at 8 o'clock, P. M., at such place as the Grand Council may designate.

The records of the proceedings of the last Annual Grand Council and of any subsequent Special Grand Council shall be read, unless dispensed with.

Sec. 2. After the records are approved, the Most Illustrious Grand Sovereign shall appoint a *Committee on Credentials*, composed of three members of this Grand Council, who shall report the name of each Representative present, as well as the names of those for whom they are to act.

Sec. 3. The following Standing Committees, each to consist of three members, shall be appointed, who shall report upon the several matters referred to them during the session:

On the Doings of the Grand Officers.
On Dispensations and Charters.
On By-Laws.
On Finance, including the Grand Treasurer's and Grand Recorder's accounts.
On Grievances and Appeals.
On Designating the Next Place of Meeting.
On Unfinished Business.
On Mileage and Pay of Representatives.
On Jurisprudence and Ritual.
On Foreign Correspondence.
On Printing and Publishing.

SEC. 4. The election for Grand Officers shall be held on the morning of the second day of the session, at 10 o'clock, A. M. The appointed officers shall be announced by the Most Illustrious Grand Sovereign immediately preceding his installation.

SEC. 5. The several Grand Officers shall hold their respective offices until their successors shall be duly elected and installed.

SEC. 6. All questions shall be determined by a majority of votes, except alteration of this Constitution, which is hereafter provided for.

SEC. 7. The Grand Council shall have exclusive jurisdiction over the Knights of the Red Cross of Constantine and Appendant Orders in this State, grant charters, decide appeals, and settle all controversies that may arise between subordinate Conclaves, promulgate the Ritual prescribed by the Grand Council of England, and do all things to promote the good, well being, and perpetuation of Christian Masonry.

SEC. 8. Every resolution of the Grand Council shall become law, as well as the decisions of the Most Illustrious Grand Sovereign, if approved by the Grand Council, and be binding and conclusive, and shall be carried into effect accordingly.


## STATUTE IV.

### SPECIAL GRAND COUNCILS.

SEC. 1. A Special Grand Council may be held at any time the Most Illustrious Grand Sovereign and Most Illustrious Grand Viceroy may think fit, and which shall be convoked by the Illustrious Grand Recorder, upon thirty days' notice, signed by the Most Illustrious Grand Sovereign and Illustrious Grand Recorder, by a circular addressed to each Grand and Past Grand Officer, to each Subordinate Conclave, and to every member of this Grand Council, setting forth the business to be transacted.

SEC. 2 Every Special Grand Council, after having been opened, shall proceed to the consideration of the business for which it shall have been convoked, and no other business shall be discussed or transacted.

## STATUTE V.

### DUTIES OF OFFICERS.

### MOST ILLUSTRIOUS GRAND SOVEREIGN.

SEC. 1. The Most Illustrious Grand Sovereign shall be elected for the term of one year, and may be re-elected.

SEC. 2. The Most Illustrious Grand Sovereign shall preside over all Stated and Special Councils in this jurisdiction, exercise a watchful supervision over all the Subordinate Conclaves, and see that all the constitutional enactments, rules, and edicts of the Grand Council of England and of this Grand Council are duly and promptly observed.

He shall have power, during the recess, to grant letters of dispensation to eleven or more petitioners, properly recommended, possessing the constitutional qualifications, empowering them to form and open a Conclave. This dispensation shall cease at the next Annual Grand Council or be continued by order of the Grand Council.

SEC. 3. No dispensation shall be issued unless the petition shall be recommended by the nearest Conclave, and the petitioners give satisfactory evidence of good standing, of a suitable place of meeting, of possessing or having the ability to procure proper furniture and dress for the use of the Conclave, and of being competent to conduct intelligently the ceremonies, work, and government thereof.

SEC. 4. He may visit and preside at any Conclave, and give such instructions and directions as the good of the Order may require, but always adhering to the ancient landmarks.

SEC. 5. The M. P. Grand Sovereign may confer the orders "at sight" for the purpose of organizing new Conclaves under dispensation and the fees therefore shall be returned to this Grand Council, and the minimum fees in such cases shall be ten dollars for each member.

## STATUTE VI.

### MOST ILLUSTRIOUS GRAND VICEROY.

SEC. 1. The M. I. Grand Viceroy in the event of the death, re-

moval or physical incompentency of his superior, shall act as the
M. I. Grand Sovereign, and exercise all the powers, authorities
and privileges given to and vested in him. At all other times
he shall perform such duties as may be assigned him by the Grand
Council, or the M. I. Grand Sovereign.

## STATUTE VII.

### ILLUSTRIOUS GRAND TREASURER.

Sec. 1. It is the duty of the Illustrious Grand Treasurer to
attend the Conclaves of the Grand Council, with the books,
papers, and properties of his office, in order to make settlement
with the committee, and pay such orders as may have been passed
by vote of the Grand Council, attested by the M. I. Grand Sovereign, and countersigned by the Grand Recorder; also, those drawn
by the Committee on Mileage and Pay of Representatives. He
shall, at each Annual Conclave, present an accurate written report
of the state of the treasury; and before entering upon the duties
of his office, give his bond to the M. I. Grand Sovereign in the
sum of $1,000. He shall receive all moneys from the hands of the
I. Grand Recorder, and give his receipt therefor, being careful to
make due entries of the same in a book to be kept for that purpose;
and, at the expiration of his office, he shall deliver over to his successor, all moneys, papers, books, and other property that may be
in his hands or under his control as Illustrious Grand Treasurer.

## STATUTE VIII.

### ILLUSTRIOUS GRAND RECORDER.

Sec. 1. The Illustrious Grand Recorder shall attend all Conclaves of the Grand Council. He shall make an annual report of
the returns of the subordinate Conclaves, showing their elected
officers, the increase and numbers, and the amount paid or due by
them; prepare and cause to be printed, a roll of the members of this
Grand Council, which shall be distributed in the Grand Council

at its first session, subject to amendment, which list when amended shall be used to designate the votes in this Grand Body, also such other matters as may conduce to the general good of the Order.

SEC. 2. He shall keep a true record of the proceedings of this Grand Council, and receive and collect all moneys due from the subordinate Conclaves, and pay the same over to the Illustrious Grand Treasurer forthwith, taking his receipt therefor.

SEC. 3. He shall transmit to the officers of the Grand Council of England, to the M. I. Grand Sovereign and I. Grand Recorder of each State Grand Council, and to the Recorder of each subordinate Conclave under this jurisdiction, copies of our annual proceedings. He shall keep in a suitable book, a register of each subordinate Conclave, showing the present and past officers and members of each ; also, all rejections, suspensions, and admissions, deaths, resignations, and those degraded.

SEC. 4. He shall transmit to the Recorder of each Conclave, the names of all candidates rejected, Knights suspended or degraded, within this jurisdiction, once every month.

SEC. 5. He shall have his books, papers and accounts present at the opening of each Annual Conclave, prepared for settlement with the Committee of the Grand Council; and at the expiration of his term of office, deliver over to his successor, all property or other matters in his hands belonging to the Grand Council.

SEC. 6. All official communications shall have the seal of the Grand Council affixed thereto.

SEC. 7. For his services he shall receive a compensation to be fixed annually.

SEC. 8. He shall notify every member of the Grand Council of the Annual and Special Conclaves of this Grand Council.

## STATUTE IX.

### DUTIES OF COMMITTEES.

#### On the doings of the Grand Officers.

They shall have charge of all the reports of the Grand Officers, with the documents referred to, and report by resolution or otherwise, what action should be taken in the premises by the Grand Council.

### On Charters and Dispensations.

They shall particularly examine the work and records of the Conclaves under Dispensation, and report to the Grand Council such action as they shall deem proper in the premises.

### On By-Laws.

They shall report all matters that are improper or unconstitutional in any By-Laws, and submit the same to the Grand Council with such recommendation as they shall deem proper.

### On Finance.

It shall be their duty to examine the books and vouchers of the Illustrious Grand Treasurer and Illustrious Grand Recorder, settle and balance the same, and report to the Grand Council the actual condition of the finances. All applications for a remission of fees and dues by subordinate Conclaves shall be referred to this Committee, who shall report thereon to the Grand Council. They shall report an estimate of the receipts and expenditures, and the necessary appropriations for the next year.

### On Grievances and Appeals.

All matters of controversy and grievance brought before the Grand Council shall be referred to this Committee, whose duty it shall be to examine into the same, and report their action thereon to the Grand Council.

### On designating the next Place of Meeting.

Their duty shall be to designate a place for the next Annual Conclave.

### On Unfinished Business.

It shall be their duty to examine the record of the previous Annual Grand Council, and report all such matters as were then pending and undetermined.

## On Mileage and Pay of Representatives.

It shall be their duty to ascertain and report the actual traveling expenses and per diem compensation allowed the Representatives of the Grand Council, for which they shall draw warrants on the Illustrious Grand Treasurer, signed by a majority of the committee, and attested by the Most Illustrious Grand Sovereign.

### On Jurisprudence and Ritual.

To them shall be referred all propositions to revise, alter, or amend the Statutes and regulations of the Grand Council, as well as all other matters on questions of law or usage, or the Ritual, and they shall report thereon, in writing, as far as proper, to the Grand Council.

### On Foreign Correspondence.

They shall have charge of so much of the Most Illustrious Grand Sovereign's address as relates to matters of foreign correspondence, together with the proceedings of the parent or sister Grand Councils, with the documents referred to, and report to the Grand Council. They shall select such portions of the proceedings of the Grand Council as are proper for publication, which, together with the report on Foreign Correspondence and statistical table, shall be published.

### On Printing and Publishing.

They shall have the exclusive control of all printing for and on account of the Grand Council, which they shall award to the lowest and best bidder.

## STATUTE X.

### FEES, DUES.

SEC. 1. Each Grand Officer and Representative from a subordinate Conclave shall be entitled to receive his actual traveling and per diem expenses for each day necessarily spent in attending the Conclaves of the Grand Council.

Sec. 2. The revenue of the Grand Council shall be derived from the following sources:

For every dispensation, to be paid before the same is is-
sued,        .        .        .        .        .        .        .        $50 00
For every Knight receiving either or all of the Orders of
Knighthood,        .        .        .        .        .        .        .        2 00
For annual dues,        .        .        .        .        .        .        .        25

Sec. 3. The initiation fee of two dollars shall be immediately forwarded to the Illustrious Grand Recorder, who shall forthwith issue a Grand Council certificate.

Sec. 4. For a dispensation for the Most Puissant Sovereign and Viceroy, three dollars each.


## STATUTE XI.

### SUBORDINATE CONCLAVES.

Sec. 1. Every Conclave shall assemble at least quarterly for business.

Sec. 2. Each Conclave shall hold its annual election at the stated conclave preceding St. John's Day in December, and the installation of officers shall take place on or before St. John's Day.

Sec. 3. Every Conclave shall, before St. John's Day in each year, transmit to the Illustrious Grand Recorder, in such form as shall be furnished, its annual return, accompanied by the fees and dues to the Grand Council. The year commences on December 27, and all documents to be dated from A. O. 313.

Sec. 4. Any Conclave neglecting or refusing to make its annual returns on or before December 27, accompanied by fees and dues, shall be notified thereof; and if after three months' notice it fail to pay, it shall be suspended until restored by a vote of the Grand Council.

Sec. 5. Any Conclave which shall omit to make its annual returns and payments on or before the first Thursday of February, shall thereby be deprived of its representation in the Grand Council.

Sec. 6. When a Conclave is disbanded or dissolved, by neglecting to make its returns, or pay its dues, or by unknightly conduct, or by the death and resignation of its members, it shall be the duty of the last Most Puissant Sovereign, Illustrious Treasurer and Recorder, within three months after its dissolution, to surrender to the Illustrious Grand Recorder the warrant, books, papers, jewels, furniture, and funds of such Conclave, together with an inventory thereof. No Knight of such Conclave shall be admitted into any other Conclave, nor entitled to the benefits of Christian Masonry, until he shall have paid to the Illustrious Grand Recorder all his arrears.

SEC. 7. The officers of a subordinate Conclave shall be—

1. A Most Puissant Sovereign, as Constantine.
2. A Viceroy, as Eusebius.
3. A Senior General.
4. A Junior General.
5. A High Prelate.
6. A Treasurer.
7. A Recorder.
8. A Prefect.
9. A Standard Bearer.
10. A Herald.
11. A Sentinel.

The elected officers shall be—

1. A Most Puissant Sovereign.
2. A Viceroy.
3. A Senior General.
4. A Junior General.
5. A High Prelate.
6. A Treasurer.
7. A Recorder.

The remaining officers shall be appointed by the Most Puissant Sovereign, immediately before his installation.

SEC. 8. A Conclave not distinguished by a name or title, being desirous of taking one, must, for that purpose, procure the approbation of the Most Illustrious Grand Sovereign, and the name must be registered with the Illustrious Grand Recorder. No Conclave is permitted to alter its name without the like approbation and registry, nor can it be named after any living person.

SEC. 9. Subordinate Conclaves may, by vote, confer the rank of honorary member upon any Knights Companion who may be deemed worthy of that distinction; and such member shall be entitled to all the privileges of an ordinary member, except that of voting.

## STATUTE XII.

### GENERAL REGULATIONS.

SEC. 1. Subordinate Conclaves shall not confer the Orders of Knighthood for a less sum than fifteen dollars.

SEC. 2. Every applicant for the Red Cross of Constantine and Appendant Orders must enclose the whole amount of the fee before the Orders are conferred.

SEC. 3. Every applicant for the Orders of Knighthood must apply by petition at a stated assembly, at least one month prior to his reception, recommended by two Knights, members of the Conclave, such petition stating his age, occupation, residence, and Commandery of Knights Templar, and that he has not been rejected by any other regular Conclave. Every such applicant must at the time of his application be a member in good standing of a Commandery of Knights Templar. A committee of investigation, of three Knights, members of the Conclave, neither of whom is a recommender, shall be appointed on such application, who reporting favorably, the applicant is ballotted for on a stated night of assembly, and receiving a unanimous vote, is declared to be approved.

SEC. 4. An applicant for the Orders of Knighthood or membership may withdraw his petition before report made thereon, or afterwards, if the report be favorable.

SEC. 5. If an applicant be rejected, a second ballot may be had on the motion of any member, duly seconded, made at one stated assembly, and adopted at the next or some subsequent assembly within six months. But the ballot so allowed shall be taken at the next stated assembly after the adoption of such motion.

SEC. 6. An applicant being twice rejected, no further ballot in his case shall be had for the space of twelve months thereafter, when a new petition in his case may be received in usual form.

SEC. 7. The objection of any one member of the Conclave shall be sufficient to prevent the conferring of the Orders of Knighthood upon a candidate, even after approval. After having received the Order of the Red Cross, his advancement shall be within the control of the Conclave.

SEC. 8. A Knight, upon written notice to the Conclave, and the payment of all dues, may withdraw, and receive a demit. An unaffiliated member loses all claim upon the Order; nor can he be admitted more than once as a visitor in a subordinate Conclave in this jurisdiction.

SEC. 9. Should the office of Most Puissant Sovereign or Viceroy of a Conclave become vacant from any cause, it shall be the duty of the Most Illustrious Grand Sovereign, upon the application of the Conclave, to issue a dispensation to authorize a special election to be held to fill such vacancy, after written or printed notice sent to every member. Such election shall not be held except at a stated assembly.

SEC. 10. An applicant for the Orders of Knighthood may apply to any Conclave within the jurisdiction, providing, should he apply to any Conclave other than the one nearest his place of residence, the Conclave nearest his place of residence shall be immediately notified of the application, and its consent obtained before conferring the Orders.

SEC. 11. The suspension or expulsion of a Knight Templar shall, *ipso facto*, cause his suspension or expulsion from his Conclave.

SEC. 12. A Knight suspended for non-payment of dues may, upon payment of the same, be restored to good standing in the Order; but to be restored to membership, he must apply in the usual manner.

SEC. 13. On the rejection of an applicant for the Orders of Knighthood, it shall be the duty of the Recorder to forthwith notify the Illustrious Grand Recorder.

SEC. 14. In all elections for officers in the Grand Council or its subordinates, a majority of the whole number of votes given is

necessary for a choice ; but if on the first ballot no choice be made,
a second shall be had, confined, where the votes are unequal, to
the two highest on the return ; and where there are three or more
candidates, one having a plurality of the votes and two or more
an equal number of votes, then confined to such candidates; and
where the votes are equal, to those having an equal number of
votes. If, on the second ballot, there be no election, the contest
between the candidates, in either of the above contingencies shall
be determined by lot.

## STATUTE XIII.

### REGALIA.

#### MEMBERS OF THE GRAND COUNCIL.

*Apron*—A white satin apron, edged with crimson silk, one inch
and a half in width ; crimson silk lining ; segmental flap, on which
the emblem of office is to be embroidered ; embroidered cross, &c.,
in the centre of apron, (see Engraving No. 1;) Greek *A* on the
right side and Greek *Ω* embroidered in green silk on the left side.
Gold fringe to apron.

No. 1.

No. 2.

*Sash*—Crimson on silk, four inches wide, edged with gold lace,
one inch in width. Emblem of office embroidered with gold on
green silk, in front of the sash.

*Sword*—Cross-hilted, and with crimson sheath.

*Jewel*—(See Engraving No. 2.) To be suspended from a crimson ribbon, one inch in width, edged with gold fringe.

For emblems of office to be placed on flap of Grand Sovereign's and Grand Viceroy's aprons, see Engravings Nos. 6 and 7 respectively.

*No. 6.*

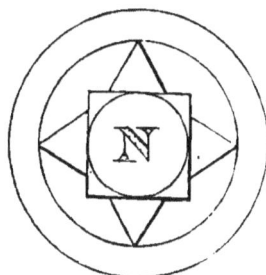

*No. 7.*

## KNIGHTS OF THE GRAND CROSS.

*Apron, Sash and Sword*—The same as above, using purple, instead of crimson.

*Jewel*—The same as No. 3, with radiating rays from the centre.

*No. 3.*

*No. 4.*

## SOVEREIGNS AND PAST SOVEREIGNS.

*Apron and Sash*—Same as members of Grand Council, omitting the gold fringe, but having a crown on the flap, with the Greek letters.

*Sword*—As above.

*Jewel*—Omitting radiated circle.

## VICEROY AND PAST VICEROYS.

*Apron and Sash*—Similar to that of a Sovereign, with mitre embroidered in gold, instead of crown on flap, without Greek letters.

*Sash, Sword and Jewel*—The same as Sovereign.

## MEMBERS OF SUBORDINATE CONCLAVES.

*Apron*—White lamb skin, edged with black ribbon one inch and a quarter wide; black silk lining; cross in centre, measuring four inches each way. (See Engraving No. 5.)

*Sash*—Black silk, four inches in width.

*Sword*—Cross-hilted, black sheath.

*Jewel*—(See Engraving, No. 5.)

No. 5.

## INTENDANTS GENERAL OF DIVISIONS.

*Apron*—Similar to that adopted by the Grand Council, but green silk fringe, instead of gold, with emblem on flap; same embroidery on centre of apron, minus the crown.

*Sash*—Green fringe, instead of gold lace.

*Jewel*—As members of Grand Council.

Any subordinate Council is hereby authorized to use a purple tunic, with a red cross on the breast, for the apron usually worn, by obtaining the consent of the Most Illustrious Grand Sovereign.

*Collar of Grand Sovereign.*

*No. 8.*

*Patriarch.*

*No. 9.*

*Member of the Council.*

*No. 10.*

*Officer.*

*No. 11.*

*Knight.*

*No. 12.*

3

# STATUTE XIV.

## AMENDMENTS.

Every proposed alteration or amendment of these Statutes shall be in writing, and referred to the Committee on Jurisprudence and Ritual, who shall report at the next Annual Meeting; and it shall require a majority of the members present to adopt the same.

# DRAFT OF BY-LAWS

# SUBORDINATE CONCLAVES.

---

## STATUTE I.

### Title.

Conclave, No.     , Masonic Knights of Red Cross of Constantine and Appendant Orders of Pennsylvania.

## STATUTE II.

### Conclaves.

SEC. 1. The stated assemblies of this Conclave shall be on the of every month, except July and August, which shall be left to the discretion of the Most Puissant Sovereign.

SEC. 2. The hours of assembling shall be at       o'clock P M. from the 25th of March to the 25th of September, and at o'clock from the 25th of September to the 25th of March.

SEC. 3. No business shall be transacted at a special assembly other than that for which it was called.

## STATUTE III.

### Officers.

SEC. 1. The elective officers shall be the Most Puissant Sovereign, Viceroy. Senior General, Junior General, High Prelate, Treasurer. Recorder, and three Trustees, who shall be separately elected by ballot at the stated assembly in December.

Sec. 2. No member shall be entitled to vote at the annual election, or be eligible to any office, whose dues are not paid in full, unless the same shall have been previously remitted.

Sec. 3. All the officers of this Conclave shall be installed at the stated assembly in December, on or before St. John's Day, and shall continue in office until their successors are duly elected and installed.

## STATUTE IV.

### Duties of Officers.

Sec. 1. The *Most Puissant Sovereign* shall cause the rules and regulations of this Conclave to be duly observed, as also the Constitution of the Grand Council of this State and of the Grand Imperial Council of England; also cause accurate records of this Conclave to be kept, and just accounts rendered, and have regular returns made to the Illustrious Grand Recorder, and the annual dues promptly paid.

At the stated assembly in December, he shall appoint two Sir Knights, who, in conjunction with the Most Puissant Sovereign, shall audit the books of the Treasurer, Recorder, and Trustees, and make a report of such examination and of the condition of the finances of the Conclave, at the stated assembly in January. In the absence of the Most Puissant Sovereign, the Viceroy shall preside in the Conclave, and shall perform the duties of his station.

Sec. 2. The *Treasurer* shall keep a true and correct account of the funds of the Conclave, and submit the same, with his vouchers, annually to the Auditing Committee. He shall pay no moneys except in pursuance of a resolution of the Conclave, and upon an order signed by the Most Puissant Sovereign, and attested by the Recorder.

Sec. 3. The *Recorder* shall keep accurate records of the transactions of this Conclave, collect all moneys due the same, and pay it forthwith to the Treasurer, taking his receipt therefor. He shall issue notices for each stated and special assembly, in which, if for a stated assembly, shall be set forth the name, age, occupation, and residence of every applicant for the Orders of Knighthood or membership, together with his or their recommenders, and the committee to whom referred. He shall render returns to the Illustrious Grand Recorder of the membership and the work of the Conclave, immediately after the stated assembly in December. At the time of issuing notices for the stated assembly in December, he shall notify each member of the amount of his indebtedness, and perform such other duties appertaining to his office as the Conclave may direct; and for his services shall receive              dollars ($      ) per annum.

SEC. 4. The *Senior and Junior General, High Prelate, Prefect, Standard Bearer, Herald,* and *Sentinel* shall perform such duties as are prescribed by the ritual of the Order.

SEC. 5. The *Sentinel* shall attend every assembly of the Conclave, deliver the notices for the same, and for his services shall receive dollars ($      ) for each assembly.

SEC 6. The *Trustees* shall invest such moneys as may be placed in their hands for that purpose, in the name of " THE TRUSTEES OF             CONCLAVE, No        . MASONIC KNIGHTS OF THE RED CROSS OF CONSTANTINE, OF                     ," the Conclave to determine the nature of such investments. The Trustees shall make an annual detailed report of the funds at the stated meeting in January, and whenever ordered by the Conclave.

## STATUTE V.

### Petitions.

SEC. 1. Petitions for the Orders of Knighthood, or membership only, shall be in writing, signed in full by the applicant, recommended by two Sir Knights, members of this Conclave, such petitioner stating his age, residence, occupation, as well as the Commandery to which he belongs. The Most Puissant Sovereign shall appoint a committee of three to examine into his character, &c., and report at the next stated assembly, or as early as practicable thereafter; if the report be unanimously in favor of the applicant, he may be ballotted for.

SEC. 2. All petitions shall be accompanied by the fees, as set forth in Statute VII respectively. If the petition be withdrawn or the candidate rejected, the money shall be returned; but if approved or elected, and said petitioner does not come forward within six months thereafter, it shall be forfeited to the Conclave.

## STATUTE VI.

### Rejections.

SEC. 1. In case of the rejection of an applicant for the Orders of Knighthood or membership, no member or visitor shall disclose the name of the member who opposed the candidate, under the penalty, if a member. of expulsion; or if a visitor, of his never being permitted to visit this Conclave again, or become a member thereof; and the Most Puissant Sovereign, immediately after the rejection of any candidate, shall cause this article to be read in the hearing of all present.

Sec. 2. An applicant for the Orders of Knighthood rejected in this Conclave shall be entitled to a second ballot, due notice thereof being given by the Recorder; and if then rejected, no further ballot shall be had for the space of six months thereafter, when a new petition in his case may be received in the usual form.

## STATUTE VII.

### Fees.

The fees for conferring the Orders of Knighthood or membership shall invariably be paid in advance, and shall be as follows:

For conferring the Orders of Knight of the Red Cross of Constantine, . . . . . . . . $

For conferring the Orders of Knight of the Holy Sepulchre and St. John of Jerusalem, . . . .

Admission of a Sir Knight, . . .

## STATUTE VIII.

### Dues and Life Membership.

Sec. 1. Every Sir Knight other than a life member shall pay the sum of dollars ($   ) per annum.

Sec. 2. Any member being in arrears to the Conclave upon the night of the annual election. and neglecting or refusing to pay the same, after he has been duly notified of the proposed action of the Conclave thereon. may be suspended from membership, unless it appears that he has been absent from his place of residence six months, or has had his dues remitted: *Provided, however,* That before any member be suspended. it shall satisfactorily appear to the Conclave that such member has received due notice, as required by Sec. 3, Art. IV, of these By-Laws, or that it was impossible to serve him with such notice.

Sec. 3. Any member of this Conclave who shall pay, over and above the amount of his dues, the sum of   dollars, or. if he has been a contributing member for five consecutive years, the sum of dollars, over and above all arrearages, may, by a vote of the Conclave, be constituted a life member, and exempt from all further dues.

## STATUTE IX.

### Unknightly Conduct.

SEC. 1. That in the event of any Knight Companion offending against the Statutes or otherwise conducting himself in a discreditable manner or endeavoring to foment disunion or dissension in the Conclave, the M. P. Sovereign shall be empowered to arraign him before a committee of Griev-ance, consisting of three members, who shall hear, and report the testimony, and also, decide whether he is worthy or not to remain a member of this christian and chivalric fraternity.

SEC. 2. If charges are preferred against a Sir Knight, the same course shall be pursued.

## STATUTE X.

### Resignations.

Any member wishing to resign shall give his notice in writing at a stated. assembly, pay his entire indebtedness to the Conclave, when his resignation shall be placed upon the minutes, and be acted upon at the next stated assembly. If the Sir Knight is required to leave the place of his residence, his resignation may be accepted forthwith.

## STATUTE XI.

### Amendments.

Any amendment or alteration to these By-Laws must be presented in writing at a stated assembly; if seconded, it shall be read by the Recorder and entered on the minutes, and lie over until the next assembly, when it shall require the vote of a majority of the members present, to amend, repeal, or enact any such law or laws: *Provided,* That the members have been duly notified that such alteration is to be acted upon.

# FORMS.

---

## No. 1.

### Form of Petition for Dispensation to Establish a Council.

*To the Most Illustrious Grand Sovereign of Knights of the Red Cross of Constantine and the Appendant Orders of the State of Pennsylvania.*

The petition of the undersigned respectfully represents that they are severally Knights of the Red Cross of Constantine and Appendant Orders, residing in the Commonwealth of Pennsylvania, that they are in good standing as Knights of these Illustrious Orders, and among them are, in their opinion, a competent number, well qualified to form and open a Conclave of Knights of the Red Cross of Constantine, and the Appendant Orders, and to properly discharge the various duties thereof, according to ancient usage; that they have a suitable place of meeting, and ability to procure proper furniture and dress for conducting the ceremonies and work of Conclave. Having the good of the Order at heart, and desirous to extend the benefits and blessings thereof to worthy Knight Companions, they pray for a dispensation empowering them to form, open, and hold a regular Conclave of Knights of the Red Cross of Constantine, and the Appendant Orders in the                    of                    , county of                    , and State of Pennsylvania, to be named                    Conclave, subordinate to, under the jurisdiction of and to be conducted in accordance with the Statutes, Rules and Edicts of the Grand Council of Pennsylvania, the Grand Imperial Council of England, and the general principles, customs, and usages of the Order

And they beg leave respectfully to recommend Eminent Sir                    as the first M. P. Sovereign, Sir                    as the first Viceroy, or Eusebius.

Dated,                    , A. D. 18    , A. O 15

(Signed)

## No. 2.

### Recommendation of the nearest Conclave.

*( To be attached to the Petition for Dispensation.)*

At a Stated Assembly of the Knights of        Council
No.     . Knights of the Red Cross of Constantine, stationed at
       , Pennsylvania. held on the      day of
   , A∘ D. 18   , A. L. 58   . A. O. 15    , on motion duly made
and seconded, it was

*Resolved,* That the petition of the foregoing Knights for a dispensation
for a new Conclave at        be recommended to the favorable consideration of the M. Illustrious Grand Sovereign. this being the
nearest Conclave.

[SEAL.]

                                          *M. P. Sovereign.*

Attest:                           *Recorder.*


## No. 3.

### Dispensation to Open a New Conclave.

*To all whom it may concern—Greeting:*

*Whereas,* A petition of sundry Knights of the Red Cross of Constantine and the Appendant Orders, in the       of
praying that a dispensation may be granted them to open and hold a Conclave of Knights of the Red Cross and the Appendant Orders, at the
     of       in the county of        , and
aforesaid, has been presented to me for consideration :

*And whereas,* It appears to me that the prayer of the petitioners ought
to be granted :

*Now, know ye,* That I           Most Illustrious Grand Sovereign of the Grand Council of Knights of the Red Cross of Constantine
and the Appendant Orders for the State of Pennsylvania, by virtue of the
power in me vested, do grant this, my dispensation, to
   , the petitioners aforesaid, and to their associates and successors, and
empower them to open and hold a Council of Knights of the Red Cross
and of the Appendant Orders, at the place aforesaid, to be called and distinguished by the name of         Council, No.     , and in

each of the several Orders to confer the respective degrees thereof upon such Knights Templar, possessing the requisite qualifications, as they may think proper.

*And I do, by these presents,* appoint Eminent Sir as Most Puissant Sovereign, and Eminent Sir as Viceroy, with continuance to them of said powers and privileges, until the Thursday after the second Wednesday of February, in the year of our Lord, one thousand eight hundred and , and no longer; as which time they are hereby enjoined to make a return of this dispensation, *with all their official doings under the same : Provided, nevertheless,* That the said officers and members of said Council, pay due respect to our said Grand Council, and to the Statute and edicts thereof, and in no way remove the ancient landmarks of our Order; or otherwise, this dispensation and all things therein contained, to be void and of no effect.

Given under my hand and seal of the Grand Council, at the of , this day of , in the year of our Lord, eighteen hundred and .

*M. I. Grand Sovereign.*

Attest: *I. Grand Recorder.*

## No. 4.

### Form of Charter.

*Most Illustrious Grand Sovereign.*

*To all worthy Eminent and Perfect Knights of the Illustrious Order of the Red Cross of Constantine, the Invincible Order of Knights of the Holy Sepulchre, and of the Holy Order of St. John.*

IN THE NAME OF THE BLESSED TRINITY IN UNITY.

*FAITH.*          *UNITY.*          *ZEAL.*

*Greeting:*

Know Ye.

That we the Most Illustrious Grand Council of the said Illustrious and Ancient Orders do hereby authorize and empower our trust, and well beloved Sir Knights

to open and hold a Royal and Imperial Conclave of the Red Cross and

Appendant Orders at                              in the                              of
and State of Pennsylvania, to be designated
Conclave, No.

And there to admit, receive, constitute and install according to Ancient
Custom such Knight Templars as may be deemed worthy of the Honor
of Knighthood in our Christian and Chivalric Fraternity.

And we do further nominate and appoint the Eminent Sir Knight
to be the First *Most Puissant Sovereign* and

Eminent Sir Knight
to be the *First Viceroy or Eusebius* of the said Conclave with power to
install their successors duly elected and chosen, and to invest them with
all the powers and dignities to their offices, respectively belonging, and
deliver to them the Charter of Incorporation, and such successors shall
in like manner from time to time install their successors as above directed,
*Provided always*, that the above named Knights and their successors do
render, and cause to be rendered, due respect and obedience to the General Statutes of the Order and edicts, rules and regulations of the Grand
Council, and do pay or cause to be paid annually, the stipulated fees and
contributions for each member to our Grand Recorder for the time being,
otherwise this charter to be of no force or effect.

Given in our Grand Council Chamber at the                              of
county of                              State of
Pennsylvania, and under the celestial canoply of the Zenith. Sealed with
the Grand seal of the Order, and signed by our Grand Dignitaries.

*G. V. or Eusebius.*

Attest:

*Grand Recorder.*


# No. 5.

**Form of Dispensation to elect Officers out of the Warranted Time.**

*To all true and courteous Sir Knights, but more especially to the Officers
and Members of*                              Conclave, No.              , *in the*
*of*                              , *Greeting:*

*Know ye,* That whereas no regular election of the officers of the aforesaid Conclave, under its Charter and By-Laws, took place at the time and
place as provided for in such By-Laws, to wit, for the annual election in
December last: *Now, therefore, I.*                              , M. I.

Grand Sovereign of the Grand Council of Knights of the Red Cross of Constantine, of the State of Pennsylvania, by virtue of the high powers in me vested, do hereby grant and issue this, my special dispensation, unto our worthy subordinate, the aforesaid                    Conclave, No.       , hereby authorizing the officers and members of such Conclave, at such time and place as may be by them appointed, to wit, at a regular meeting, to proceed and in due order elect suitable Sir Knights of their Conclave, to serve in the several offices provided for in their By-Laws; and the Sir Knights so elected, after being duly installed, to serve until the next annual election, and installation of its officers, under the said By-Laws; all members to have due and timely notice of such meeting and for the election, aforesaid  And I hereby enjoin it upon the Most Puissant and Recorder of such Conclave to certify under the seal of said Conclave, to our *Illustrious* Grand Recorder, within six days after said election, the proceedings had under this dispensation.

Given under my hand and seal, at                        , this day of           , A. D. 18    , A. O. 15

                                        *M. I. G. S. of G. C. of Pa.*

Attest:

                    *I. Grand Recorder.*


## No. 6.

### Special Election Return.

We, the M. P. Sovereign and Recorder of Conclave, No.      , stationed at                        , under the authority of the Grand Council of Knights of the Red Cross of Constantine of the State of Pennsylvania, do hereby certify to the Grand Council, that at an election held by virtue of a dispensation from the Most Illustrious Grand Sovereign, on the             day of           , A. D. 18    , A. O. 15    , the following Knights were duly elected officers of the said Conclave for the remainder of the present year, viz:

                    *Most Puissant Sovereign.*
                    *Viceroy.*
                    *Senior General.*
                    *Junior General.*
                    *High Prelate.*
                    *Treasurer.*
                    *Recorder.*

Witness our hands and the seal of the said Conclave, at                ,
this             day of              , A. B. 18      , A. O. 15

[SEAL.]

                                  *M. P. S.*

Attest :                          . *Recorder.*

# No. 7.

## Diploma.

*The Most Illustrious Council of Knights of the Red Cross of Constantine and Appendant Orders,*

To all True and Faithful Soldiers of the Cross :

*(in margin: Ne Varietur.)*

*Know Ye,* That the Worthy and Eminent Sir                ,
who hath signed his name in the margin hereof, was regularly admitted, received, constituted, and installed a Knight of the Red Cross
of Constantine, a Knight of the Invincible Order of the Holy Sepulchre, and a Knight of the Order of St. John, on the
day of              , A. D. 18      , A. O. 15      , in
                Conclave, No.      , located in                    .
county of                , and state of Pennsylvania, and that he
is duly enrolled in the books of the Order.

In testimony whereof, we have hereunto subscribed our names, and
affixed the seal of the Conclave, the day and year above
[SEAL.]   written.

*(in margin: (Signature ))*

                         *M. I. G. Sovereign.*
                         *M. I. G. Viceroy or Eusibius.*
Attest :             . *I. Grand Recorder.*

# No. 8.

## Form of Demit.

*To all Sir Knights of the Illustrious Order of the Red Cross of Con-
stantine and the Appendant Orders, to whom these presents may come—
Greeting :*

*(in margin: Ne Varietur.)*

*This is to certify,* That Sir                , Knight, whose
name appears in the margin of this Demit, is a Knight of the Illustrious Order of the Red Cross of Constantine and Appendant Orders,
late a member of                Conclave, No,      , stationed at
                , under the jurisdiction of the Most Illustrious

Grand Council of Pennsylvania. That he is in good standing in the Order, and free from all charges; and as such we courteously recommend him to the fraternal regard of all valiant and magnanimous Knights, wherever dispersed around the globe.

In testimony whereof, we have hereunto set our hands and caused the seal of our Conclave to be affixed, this

[SEAL.]　day of　　　　　　　, in the year of our Lord, 18　　,
　　　　　and of the Order 15　　.

(Signature.)

　　　　　　　　　　　　　　　*M. P. Sovereign.*
　　　　　　　　　　　　　　　*Viceroy.*

Attest:　　　　　　　　　, *Recorder.*

## No. 9.

### Form of a Certificate for Proxy.

*To the Grand Council of the State of Pennsylvania:*

*This is to certify,* That in consideration of the confidence I repose in the courtesy and magnanimity of our valiant Sir Knight
　　　　　　. I have nominated and appointed, and by these presents do nominate and appoint, the said Sir Knight　　　　　　　　　,
to be my proxy in the Grand Council of the State of Pennsylvania, then and there to represent me, and to do every act and thing agreeably to the Statutes of the Grand Council, as fully and completely as I could do myself, were I personally present.

Witness my hand and seal of　　　　　　　Conclave, No.　　,
　　　this　　　　　　day of　　　　, A. D. 18　　,
[SEAL.]　A. O. 15　　.

　　　　　　　　　　　　　　　(Name.)
　　　　　　　　　　　　　　　(Office.)

## No. 10.

### Petition for Membership.

*To the M. P. Sovereign, Officers, and Knights of*

*Conclave, No.　　, Knights of the Red Cross of Constantine and the Appendant Orders:*

The petition of the undersigned respectfully represents: That he is a Knight of the Illustrious Order of the Red Cross of Constantine, a

Knight of the Invincible Order of the Holy Sepulchre, and a Knight of the Order of St. John, late a member of Conclave, No.

He therefore prays that he may be admitted to membership in your Conclave, if on inquiry he should be found worthy.

A. D. 18   , A. O. 15

RECOMMENDED AND VOUCHED FOR ON THE HONOR OF A KNIGHT, BY

(Signed)

Age,

Occupation,

Residence,

Lodge,

Chapter,

Commandery,

No. 11.

**Report of Co mittee.**

*No.*   .

PETITION OF

*Sir*

FOR MEMBERSHIP.

*Presented*      *A. D 18   , A. O. 15*

*Committee:*

To the *M. P. Sovereign, Officers, and Sir Knights of* Conclave, *No.* , *Knights of the Red Cross of Constantine and Appendant Orders :*

The undersigned, the committee to whom was referred the foregoing application, respectfully report, that they have found the particulars set

forth in the petition to be correct, and the petitioner          worthy of
having his prayer granted.

.          ,

}
} *Committee.*
}
}

. 18    .          '

Ballotted for                    , 18    ,
and

## No. 12.

### For Dubbing and Membership.

*To the M. P. Sovereign, Officers, and Knights of*
*Conclave, No.        . Knights of the Red Cross of Constantine and the*
*Appendant Orders:*

I, the undersigned, hereby declare, that I am a Knight Templar, in
good standing, a member of              Commandery, No.    ;
a Cryptic Mason, a member of              Council, No.    ;
a Royal Arch Mason, a member of              Chapter,
No.    ; a Master Mason, a member of              Lodge,
No.    ; that I have a firm and steadfast belief in the truth of the
Christian religion and the doctrine of the Holy Trinity, as revealed in
the New Testament; that I have never been rejected in any other Conclave of Knights of the Red Cross of Constantine, and respectfully pray
that I may be admitted in your Conclave, a Knight of the Order of
Knights of the Red Cross of Constantine and Appendant Orders, and
become a member of your Conclave.

Should my request be granted, I promise to conform to all the ceremonies, engagements, rules and statutes of your Conclave.

Witness my hand, this          .          day of          , A. D.
18    , A. O. 18    .

RECOMMENDED AND VOUCHED / (Signed.)
   FOR ON THE HONOR OF A ⌈ Age,
   KNIGHT, BY                          ⟨ Occupation,
                          ) Residence.
                          ⌈ Lodge, No.
                          ⟨ Chapter, No.
                          ( Council, No.
                          \ Commandery, No.

# No. 13.

## Report of Committee.

*No.* .

PETITION OF

*Sir Knight*

FOR DUBBING AND MEMBERSHIP

*Presented* , *A. D. 18* . *A O. 18*

*Committee :* (

To the *M. P. Sovereign, Officers, and Sir Knights of*
No. , *Knights of the Red Cross of Constantine and*
*Appendant Orders :*

The undersigned, the committee to whom was referred the foregoing
application. respectfully report, that they have found the particulars set
forth in the petition to be correct, and the petitioner worthy of
having his piayer granted.

} *Committee.*

18 .

Ballotted for 18 .
and

## No. 14.

### Form of Returns from Subordinate Conclaves.

*A list of Contributing Members of*    *Conclave, No.*    *, held at*    *, and State of Pennsylvania, from December 27, A. D. 18*    *. A. O. 15*    *.*

*county of*    *, A. O. 15*    *.*

*to December 27, A. D 18*    *.*

| Christian and surnames in full. | Residence. | Profession. | Commandery | Age. | Death. | Withdrn'g | Suspens'n | Expulsion |
|---|---|---|---|---|---|---|---|---|
| | | | | | | | | |